Beginner Electric Guitar Lessons

Book with Online Video & Audio Access

by
Peter Vogl

To access Online Video & Audio for this course, go to the following internet address:

cvls.com/extras/begl

Introduction

Beginner Electric Guitar Lessons Book with Online Video and Audio Access is a step-by-step course designed for beginners who want to play electric guitar. Peter Vogl will take you through all of the fundamental steps of learning to play guitar. We'll start with the basics like parts of the guitar, how to use an amp, and proper playing position. Next, we'll advance to playing chords, strum patterns, scales, and more. In addition to the content in this book, you have online access to video instruction and audio tracks that will help you learn to play correctly. These video lessons will teach you to play in rhythm and learn each concept much faster.

To access the online video and audio, go to this address on the internet:

cvls.com/extras/begl

The Author

Peter started playing guitar in 2nd grade and very quickly realized his calling. He played in several bands through his years at Okemos High, and proceeded to study classical guitar in college at the University of Georgia under the tutelage of John Sutherland. After receiving his undergraduate degree in Classical Guitar Performance Peter continued with his studies on a assistantship at James Madison University. While there he taught classes as large as 110 people at both James Madison and Mary Baldwin College.

Peter moved back to Georgia and began playing the club circuit in Atlanta as a soloist and with a multitude of bands. He also founded and managed several schools of guitar including the Guitar Learning Center. During this time Peter produced many products for Watch & Learn Inc. such as *The Guitarist's Chord Book, The Guitarist's Scale Book, Intro to Blues Guitar, Intro to Rock Guitar, The Guitarist's Tablature Book, & The Let's Jam! Series.*

In the 90's Peter met Jan Smith and began to play with the Jan Smith Band performing on several of her CDs including Nonstop Thrill, Surrender, and Resurrection. In 2001 Peter moved into Jan Smith Studios where he continues to teach and do session work with local and national talent.

Peter has performed on stage with talents such as Michael Bolton, Cee-Lo, Kelly Price, Steve Vai, Earl Klugh, Sharon Isbon, and Sleepy Brown. In collaboration with the NARAS organization he is the band leader each year at the Heroes Award Dinner in Atlanta.

Table Of Contents

Watch & Learn Products Really Work

30 years ago, Watch & Learn revolutionized music instructional courses by developing well thought out, step-by-step instructional methods that were tested for effectiveness on beginners before publication. These products, which have dramatically improved the understanding and success of beginning students, have evolved into the Watch & Learn system that continues to set the standard of music instruction today. This has resulted in sales of more than three million products since 1979. This easy to understand course will significantly increase your success and enjoyment while playing the electric guitar.

Section 1
Getting Started

To access Online Video & Audio for this course, go to the following internet address:

cvls.com/extras/begl

The Guitar

The Strings

The strings on the guitar are numbered from the bottom up or the smallest string to the highest string. 1,2,3,4,5,6. They each have a letter name or a note that they are tuned to. Starting with string number one they are E, B, G, D, A, E. This will become very important to memorize as this course progresses.

The Tuners, Nut, and Frets

The tuners are important for keeping your guitar in tune and for restringing the guitar. The Nut is where the strings first contact the guitar and the grooves in the nut allow the strings to slide through. The frets are what the strings rest on when you press down a string in a fret space. Going up the neck towards the body the pitches get higher on each string.

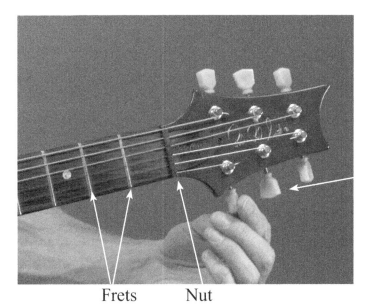

The Body

The body of the guitar is where we will find much of the electronics. The bridge is where the strings touch at this end of the guitar. The selector switch turns on one or both of the pickups. The volume dial sets the loudness of the guitar and the signal level going into the amp. This can have a profound effect on our sound. The tone dial sets the brightness or darkness of our sound. Different models of guitars will have slightly different set ups but will generally function the same. Refer to the video for more complete descriptions of different models.

Bridge

Selector   Volume   Tone   Pick ups
Switch

The Amplifier

After plugging the guitar cable into the guitar jack, plug the other end into the guitar amp. With the guitar amp still off, turn the volume completely down on the amp, plug in the guitar, turn on the amp, and then start turning up the volume. This will avoid any loud pops or accidentally turning on the amp at an extreme volume. You can strum the strings as you turn up the volume to determine the loudness you desire.

Channel Switching

Many amps come with two channels. This will enable you to play with either clean or distorted sounds. Each amp is a little bit different. The second channel may be labeled as Gain, Lead, Distortion, or just Channel 2. Since there are many possible names, check your manual. The second channel may also have two "volume" dials. On this amp they are labeled as pre gain and post gain. Remember, you also have volume dials on your guitar and if your volume dial on the guitar is not all the way up you will not hear much distortion out of your second channel. To hear distortion, make sure your volume dial on the guitar is wide open. For more details on setting up different amps refer to the video in this course.

Using a Distortion Pedal

If your amp only has one channel and no way to get distortion without turning the amp incredibly loud, you can purchase a distortion pedal. There are many varieties of these. Plug the guitar cable into one end and another guitar cable goes into the amp.

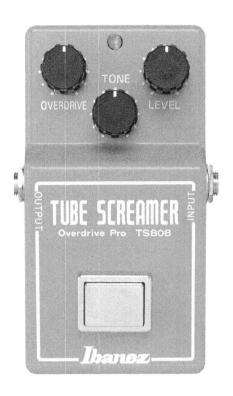

Amp Tone

Amps come with a variety of tone and knob combinations. You may have only one dial called tone or you may have two dials labeled bass and treble. In this amp, there are three dials labeled bass, mid, and treble. The bass controls the low sounds, the mid controls the middle sounds that can contribute to the warmth of the tone, and the treble controls the bright or high frequencies of the tone. A good starting position is in the middle for all of these dials or, as in this example, at 12 o'clock. If the treble knob is turned up high, your guitar might sound harsh and bright. If the bass dial is turned up too high, your guitar may sound low and muddy and the amp may rumble. Over time, you will make adjustments to your tone according to your liking. The guitar you are using will also make a huge difference in the tone you hear.

Sitting Position

For a right handed person, the guitar should be sitting on the right leg slightly leaning against the torso. The right elbow should be resting on the upper right hand corner of the guitar with the arm able to move freely. Your left arm should be able to hang from the shoulder with the thumb placed on the back of the guitar. It is usually best if both feet are able to be placed squarely on the floor. Avoid slumping or rounding the back while playing as this can cause back damage and pain over time.

Thumb Position

The pad of the left thumb should be placed on the back of the guitar neck. This position will vary according to what your hand size is, what the size of the guitar neck is, and what technique you are doing, but our "core" position will be about 50 to 75 percent up the back of the neck. The thumb pressure is generally light and able to move all directions on the neck. Pressure on the thumb increases depending on the technique. Barre chords, for example, will require much more pressure.

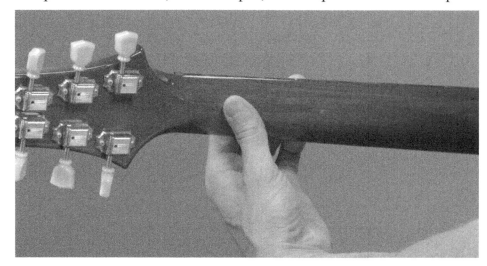

Standing Position

When standing, the guitar should hang at about the same spot on your body as if you were sitting down. Look at the height of your guitar when you are sitting and adjust your strap so that it hangs about the same height against your torso. Be sure to always keep a hand on the guitar when you are using a strap. It's also a good idea to use strap locks to keep the guitar more secure.

The Pick

I recommend most beginners start with a medium gauge pick and use the most common size. Nothing too big or small and steer away from odd shapes. As you progress, you can determine if you want to go with a heavier pick or what shape you like the best. Picks are made of different materials so they all have a slightly different tone. You will probably find a favorite pick after trying a few.

Holding The Pick

When holding the pick, place the wide part of the pick between the pad of your thumb and your index finger's first digit. This should leave you plenty of pick to play with. The other fingers are curled inward towards the palm of the hand and not extended outward. The index finger is also slightly curled in so the tip of the finger is not pointed in the same direction as the tip of the pick.

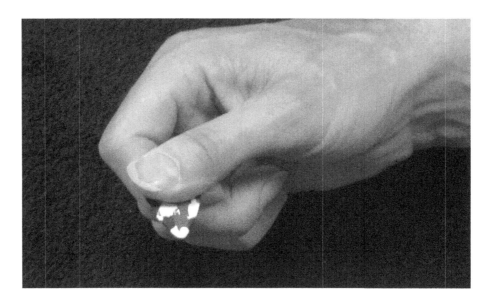

When playing, the tip of the pick should be pointed at the guitar. The index finger is curled under with the tip of the finger pointed towards the bridge pickup and not at the same angle as the guitar pick. Notice the curl of the rest of the fingers and that no other fingers are involved in holding the pick.

Strumming

When first learning to strum, there are a few positions and techniques to know. The strum is generated from the elbow down with the forearm and wrist rotating. Keep the hand, wrist, and arm relaxed. If the wrist and arm are tense, they won't rotate and the pick will collide with the strings rather than brushing them like a paint brush. Keep the strum from getting too long. A short strum is easier to control.

Correct Start Position

Correct End Position

Example

Strum the open strings with a down up motion. Below is the notation for this exercise. We'll explain how to read this later in the book.

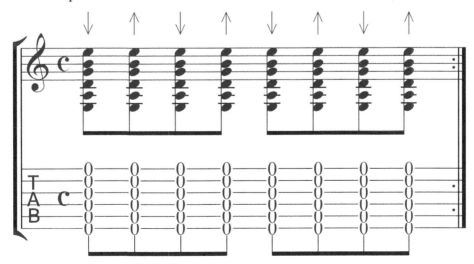

Tuning the Guitar

The most common way to tune your guitar is with either an electronic tuner or a tuning app. Luckily, most of these work the same way. If you play the 3rd string (G), you may see a G show up on the screen. If the note your string is playing is too low or flat, you might see an F or F♯. You will need to tighten your string a little until you see the G show up in the middle. If the note played by your 3rd string is too high, you may see A♭ or A. This means you need to loosen your string a little.

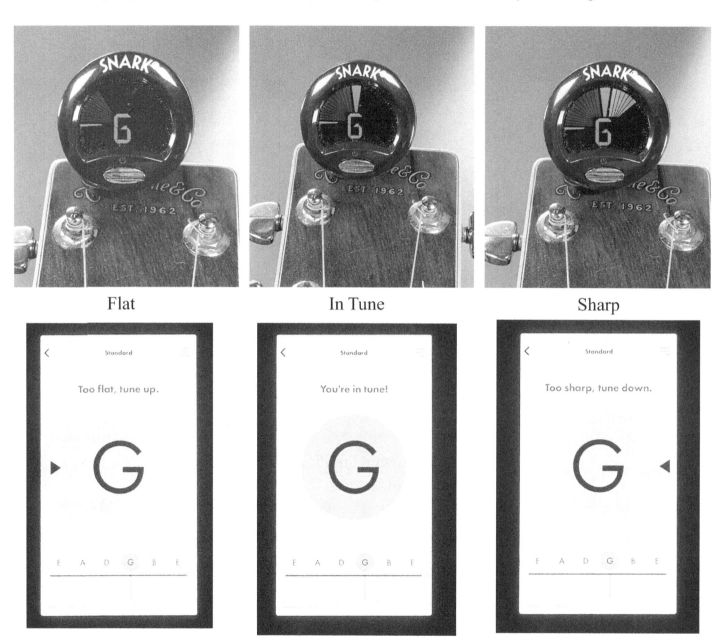

| Flat | In Tune | Sharp |

We then need to repeat this process for all six strings (E, A, D, G, B, E) until they are playing the correct note. It's important that you tune your guitar at the start of each practice session. Playing an out of tune guitar is like baking a cake with the wrong ingredients. No matter how hard you try, it won't end up tasting very good. Even famous guitarists would sound bad if they play out of tune guitars.

The Guitar Neck and the Left Hand

The metal bars on the neck of the guitar are called frets. When pressing down a string, the string rests on the crown of the fret and this is where the note is really sounded.

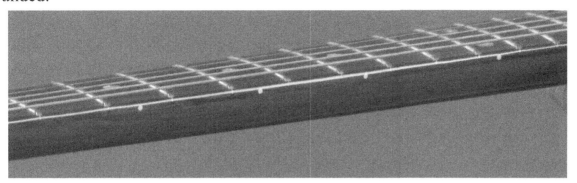

You only want to press a string down as hard as it takes to get a clean note. Pressing too hard can cause many issues. Place your finger toward the front of the fret as this is the place that requires the least amount of pressure to get a clean note. Remember, we are not pressing down the string to the wood of the guitar neck, only down to the crown of the fret which is higher than the wood.

Correct Position

Reading Tablature or Tab

Much of guitar music is written using tablature which is much easier to read than standard music notation. We will be using this method throughout this course so it is important that you learn how to read it.

The six lines of tablature represent the six strings of the guitar. The lowest line is the lowest string on the guitar or number 6 (the lowest in pitch and thickest string). The numbers on the strings represent the frets to be played. In the example below, the first number reading left to right is a zero on the sixth string. This means play an open first string with no fingers on it (only the 6th string and no others). It is written twice so you play it twice in a row.

The next number is a 4 on the 6th string, so play the 4th fret 6th string. The next number is a 2 written on the 5th string so play the 2nd fret fifth string. After that we have four numbers on the 4th string. They are 0,4,2,0. Play those frets in that order. The numbers above the tablature staff are the fingers to use. Played all together, this is a guitar riff or melody. Tablature is extremely good at writing out these sort of things. Since it is so widely used, get used to reading it.

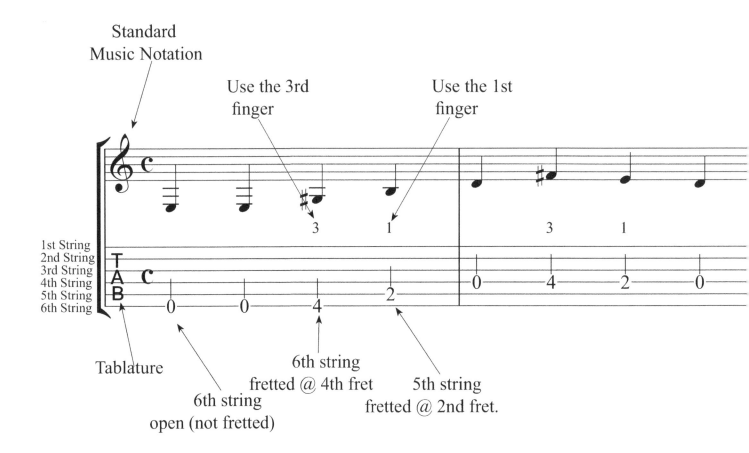

16

Left Hand Exercise

Here is a great left hand exercise to get us started. Focus on playing toward the front of the frets and good hand position.

Exercise 1

In this exercise, use frets and fingers the same. This means whatever fret you are in, that is the finger to use. In the first fret use the first finger, in the second fret use the second finger and so on. Don't worry about speed. We will work on that later.

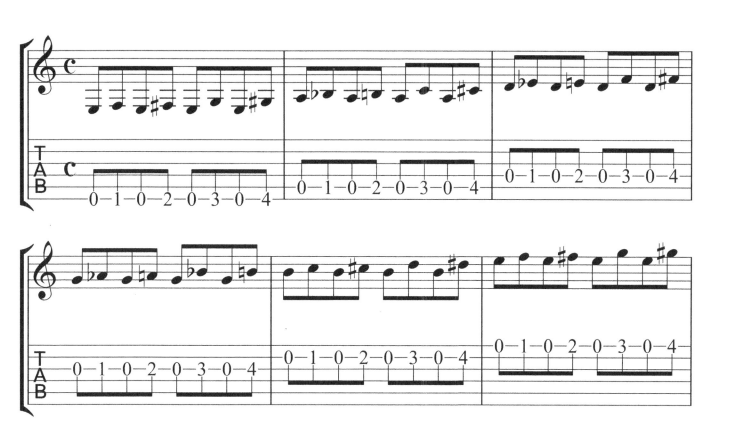

17

Em Chord

Now we can learn our first chord and make sure we understand chord diagrams.

Exercise 2

Use your first finger to press down the fifth string second fret and your second finger to press down the fourth string second fret. Keep your thumb somewhat low on the back of the neck and play on the tips of your fingers. Try not to touch any other strings with your fingers. Then strum all the strings. This chord is called E minor.

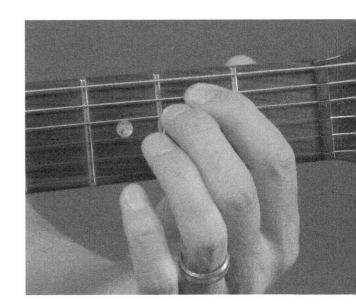

Chord Diagrams

This chord diagram represents an E minor chord, labeled Em. This little "m" stands for minor. The top thick horizontal line is the nut of the guitar neck. The horizontal lines below that are the frets. The vertical lines are the strings on the guitar with the 6th string to the left and the first string to the right. The two dots tell us where to place fingers on the guitar. They are both in the second fret with the first finger on the 5th string and the second finger on the 4th string.

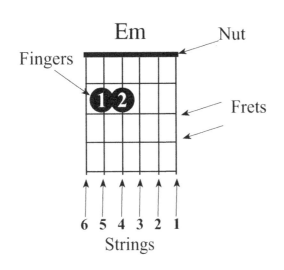

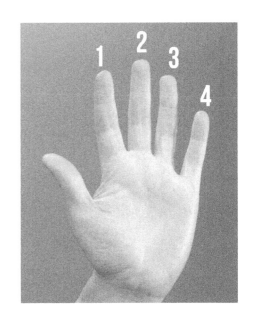

Section 2
Chords and Scales

To access Online Video & Audio for this course, go to the following internet address:

cvls.com/extras/begl

The Asus2 Chord

Here is a second chord. The Asus^2 chord. Pronounced " A sus 2". The sus is a music theory term meaning suspended.

Exercise 3

Use your second finger to press down the 4th string 2nd fret and use your 3rd finger to press down the 3rd string 2nd fret. Play on the tips of your fingers and toward the front of the frets. Strum from the fifth string down towards the floor.

Don't play this string

Asus^2

What is a Chord

We've learned a couple chords now so it's a good time to learn what a chord really is. *A chord is when you combine three or more different notes at the same time.* When we play Em we are playing the notes E-G-B. These three notes are repeated on some strings but we are only playing E-G-B.

Em

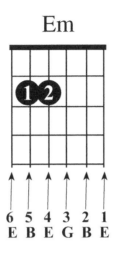

```
6   5   4   3   2   1
E   B   E   G   B   E
```

Asus2 consists of the notes A-E-B. Again some notes are repeated but these are the three notes that make up this chord.

Asus²

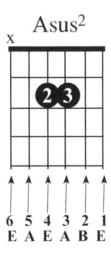

```
6   5   4   3   2   1
E   A   E   A   B   E
```

There are four *qualities* of chords. Every chord you play will be one of these. The qualities are Major, Minor, Diminished, and Augmented.

Changing Chords

The Pivot Finger

When changing from Em to Asus2, we can use a technique called a pivot finger to help us change smoothly. The 2nd finger is on the 2nd fret 4th string for both chords. This means you can leave this finger still between these chords so the 2nd finger is a pivot finger.

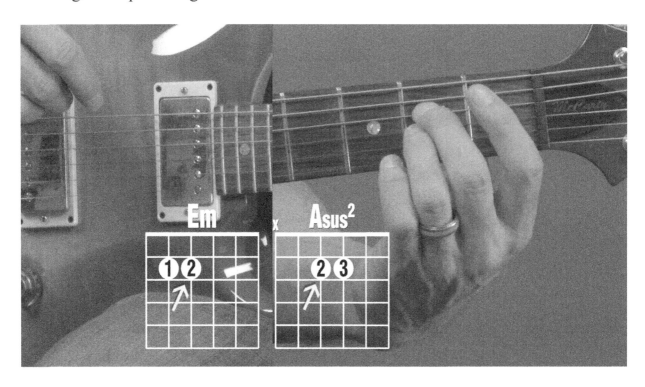

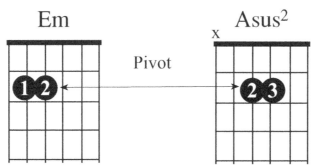

A finger that can stay still between two chords is called a pivot finger. This is one of the most important chord changing techniques you will ever learn. Whenever possible use pivot fingers to help change chords cleanly and smoothly.

Exercise 4

Practice changing from Em to Asus2 using a single downstroke on each chord. When you can do this smoothly, try playing along with the backing track provided for this exercise. This will help us learn to play in time. There is a click counting the band off and giving us the tempo of the track. Each chord lasts for four beats.

Strum once and hold for
four counts.

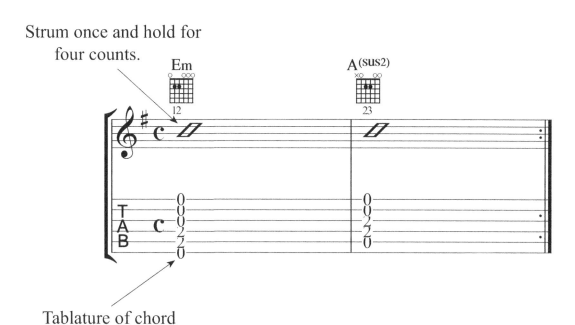

Tablature of chord

The Em Pentatonic Scale

Perhaps the most widely used scale on guitar is the pentatonic scale. We use scales to construct solos, melodies, and attach chords together. The Em pentatonic scale is a great place to start.

Exercise 5

In this exercise, we will play the Em pentatonic scale forwards. Use frets and fingers the same for the left hand. This means whatever fret you are in that is the finger to use. In the 3d fret use the 3rd finger, in the 2nd fret use the 2nd finger and so on. Practice slow and smooth.

Exercise 6

Now practice this same scale backwards.

Exercise 7

This time, practice the Em pentatonic scale forwards and backwards and don't repeat or stop on the highest note of the scale. Once you feel comfortable playing this scale, try playing along with the track. This will give you a good idea of what this scale sounds like in context. You don't have to play eighth notes or fast rhythms. Stay in time but play at a beat or subdivision you can handle. Quarter notes or half notes for example. Watch the video to get a better idea of what this means.

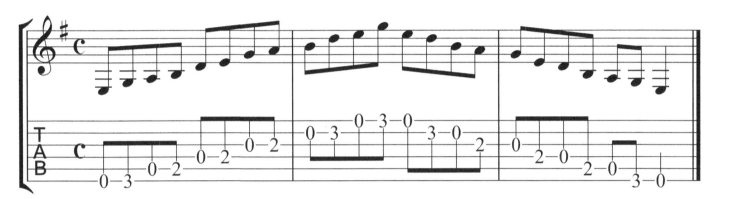

To access the online video and audio, go to this address on the internet:

cvls.com/extras/begl

Power Chords 1

Power chords are used in just about every style of music and are extremely important for electric guitar playing. First, let's make sure we can read the tablature necessary to go forward. In the example below, the 0 and 2 in the tab are stacked right on top of each other. This means play them both at the same time. The zero is on the sixth string and the two is on the fifth string. The 1 in between the staves is telling us to use the first finger on the left hand to pay the 2nd fret 5th string.

Use this finger

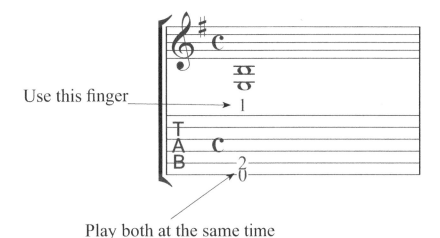

Play both at the same time

Exercise 8

This is a what we call an E power chord. Power chords are played quite often on electric guitar. When playing this chord, let your first finger lay across the strings in order to mute them. That way you won't get any extra unwanted notes. Strum just the 6th and 5th strings with your pick.

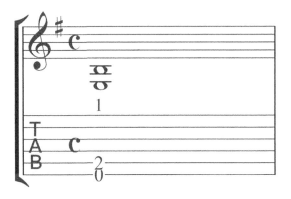

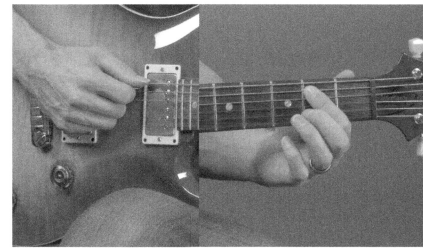

Exercise 9

This next example is an A power chord. We are now playing an open 5th string and the 2nd fret 4th string. Once again, position your index finger to lay across the open strings below this to keep from getting any unwanted notes or noise. Strum the 5th and the 6th string only.

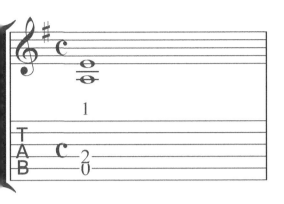

Exercise 10

Now practice changing between these two chords. When you are able to do this easily, try playing along with the track. Stay in time and listen to what these chords sound like in relation to the rest of the music. Wait for the 4 beat count off at the beginning.

Two Finger Power Chords

Playing power chords that use two fingers and no open strings will give us more flexibility. If we know power chords with a root on the 6th and the 5th strings, we can play just about any power chord we need simply by sliding up and down the neck. Let's start with two finger power chords that have a root on the 6th string.

Power Chords With a Root on the Sixth String

A power chord with a *root* on the sixth string means the note played on the sixth string names the chord. To be able to name these chords, it is important that you memorize the notes on the 6th string. The open 6th string is the note E, the 1st fret is F, the 3rd fret is G, the 5th fret is A, the 7th fret is B, the 8th fret is C, the 10th fret is D, and the 12th fret is E. The frets or notes in between are sharps and flats but for now, just memorise the notes we have labeled. These are called *natural* notes.

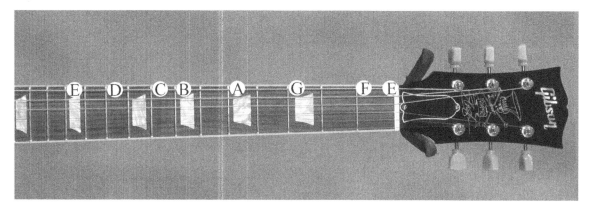

Exercise 11

These three chords, G, A, and B, all have a root on the sixth string. You might also find them named as G^5, A^5, and B^5. Practice making these chords and sliding between them. Use your 1st and 3rd fingers for all of these. Let your left index finger lay across the open strings to mute them, avoiding any extra notes or noise.

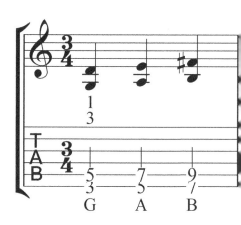

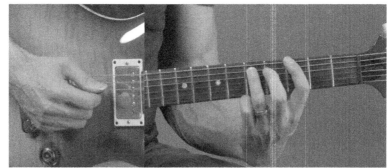

G Power Chord at 3rd fret

A Power Chord at 5th fret

B Power Chord at 7th fret

Exercise 12

Move this power chord up the neck and practice naming the chords as you go.

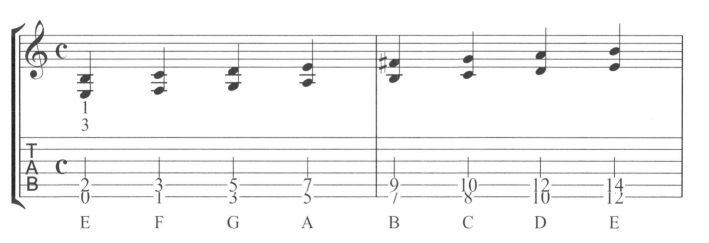

Power Chords With a Root on the Fifth String

Using the same chord shape but one string down, we can play power chords with a root on the 5th string. In order to name these chords correctly and understand them, we should first learn and memorize the notes up the 5th string just as we did the 6th string.

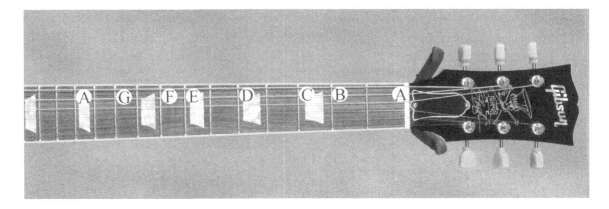

Exercise 13

These three power chords have a root on the 5th string. That means the note on the 5th string names them. Practice playing these chords and slide them around.

C Power Chord at third fret

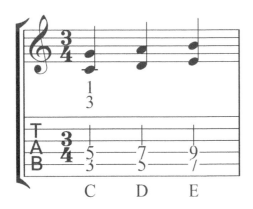

D Power Chord at fifth fret

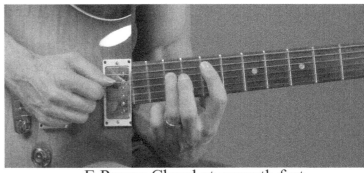
E Power Chord at seventh fret

30

Exercise 14

Move these power chords up the neck and practice naming the chords as you go.

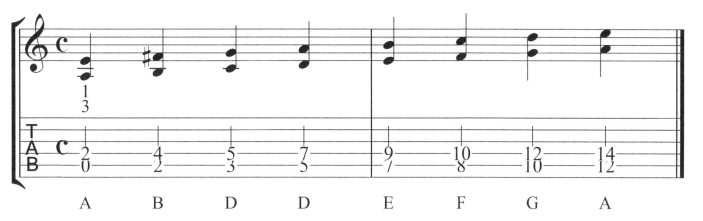

Playing With the Track

Now we can apply these shapes and practice them in a musical context.

Exercise 15

Practice these power chords in this order and then try playing with the track. Use your first and third finger throughout. Notice the first two chords in each section last for two beats with the final chord in each section lasting for four. Keep your thumb low on the back of the neck and let it slide with you as you move. Pay attention to the repeats.

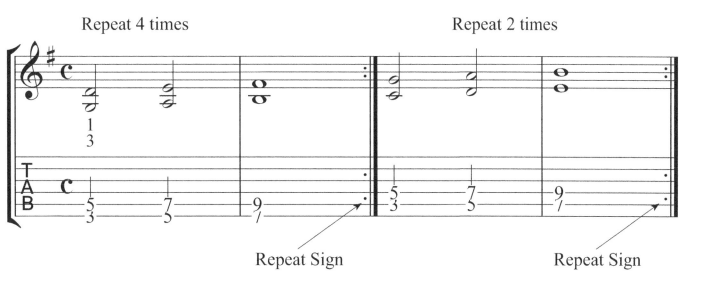

Open Position Scales

We've already learned one open position scale: the Em pentatonic scale. Now let's learn a few more. We'll start with the E Blues scale.

The E Blues Scale

The E blues scale is similar to the Em pentatonic scale and is often confused with it. Notice that the E blues scale has an extra note. This scale is used in blues as well as many other genres of music. So you'll want to become familiar with it.

Exercise 16

Practice the E blues scale forwards and backwards. Don't repeat the highest note of the scale. Simply turnaround on the highest note. Practice slowly and relaxed.

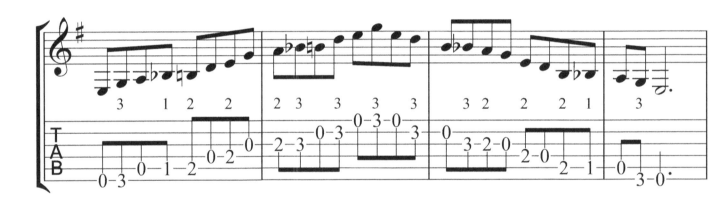

The G Major Scale

The Major scale is often called the mother of all scales. It is the scale that defines what key we are in and helps us understand music theory. The G major scale is a great example of this on the guitar.

Exercise 17

Practice the G major scale forward and backwards. This is a very important scale for future music development.

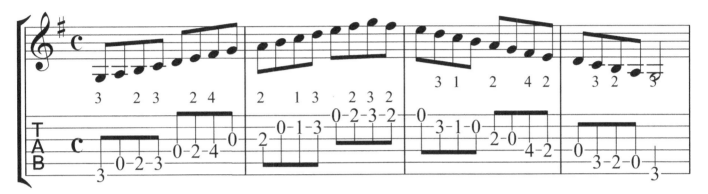

The A minor scale

Where the major scale is often thought of as a bright sound the minor scale is often though of as the polar opposite scale or a dark sound. Later it will be interesting to realize how closely they are related.

Exercise 18

Practice the A minor scale forwards and backwards. Notice how this scale starts on the open fifth string which is the note A or what is called the tonic (the note that names the scale).

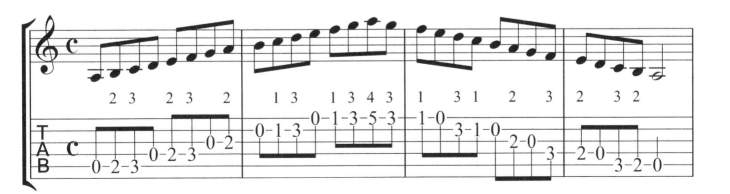

The Chromatic Scale

Chromatic means moving by half step or one fret at a time. This scale is easy to learn but actually more difficult for the hand and very good for working on finger independence and technique.

Exercise 19

Practice the Chromatic scale slowly and carefully. Pay particular attention to the third string where we break the pattern and only go up to the third fret. This way we don't repeat the note B. Keep a low thumb position to enable good hand position. Try to keep each finger floating above a fret. 1st finger above 1st fret, 2nd finger above 2nd fret, 3rd finger above 3rd fret and 4th finger above 4th fret.

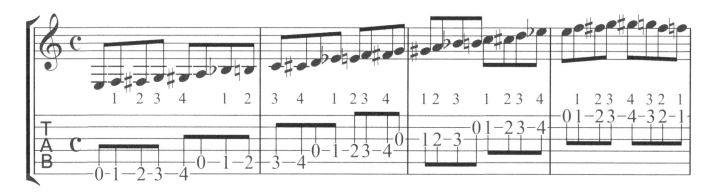

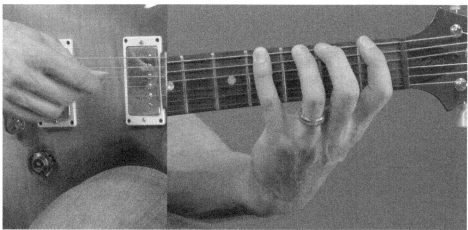

Keep each finger in fret space.

34

Alternate Picking

Alternate picking will enable us to develop our scales, solos, and melodies further. It is a more efficient and accurate technique for the right hand. Alternate picking means that when the right hand plays a scale or melody the pick will always alternate directions. Down, up, down , up, etc. Using only downstrokes or upstrokes is adding an extra motion that is slower and much more work. From this point forward our core right hand technique for playing scales, solos, and melodies will be alternate picking.

The Em Pentatonic Scale Using Alternate Picking.

Let's try this scale we have already learned but this time play every note with an opposite direction of the pick.

Exercise 20

Use alternate picking when playing this scale. Keep the pick movements small and precise. This might seem hard at first but will become much easier over time and enable better faster technique.

Pick Directions

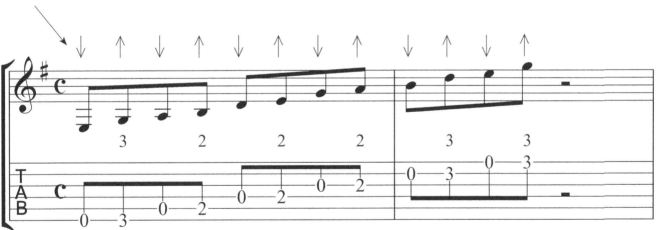

Alternate Picking Exercises

With the next couple exercises we will focus on the right hand and learning how to alternate pick. These are basic exercises that will help you get a handle on this technique.

Exercise 21

This exercise uses only the open strings so you don't need to worry about your left hand. Practice slowly at first and try to gain a feeling of where the strings are with your pick.

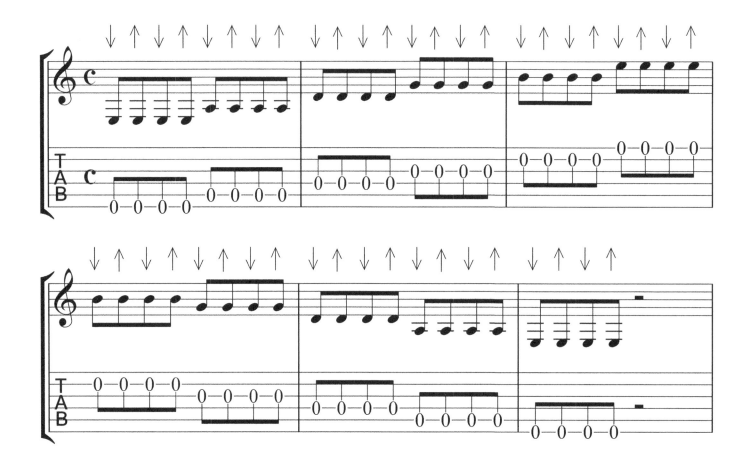

Exercise 22

This exercise is a variation of the last one. It again uses open strings but this time we are playing three times on each string. Since this is an odd number, it will cause some additional complexity to the technique. When changing strings make sure to keep the alternation going and don't repeat down or up strokes.

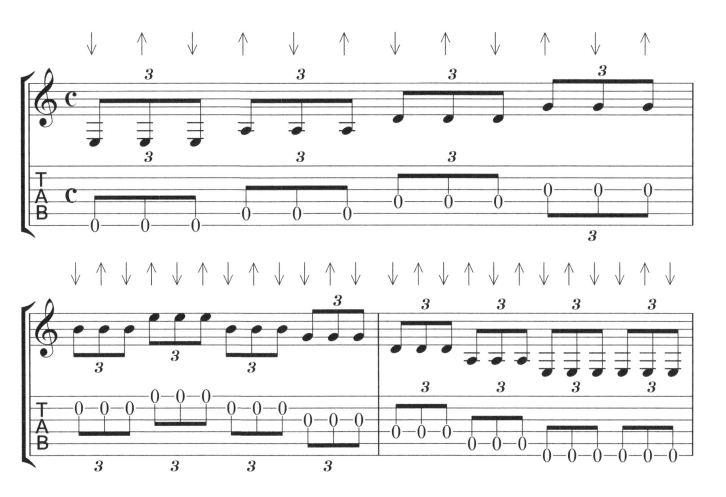

Open Scales with Alternate Picking

It's now time to apply alternate picking to the rest of our open scales.

Exercise 23

Practice the E blues scale using alternate picking. Be sure to keep the alternation going when you change strings. Pay particular attention when you are playing the scale backwards as beginners tend to repeat upstrokes on the way back.

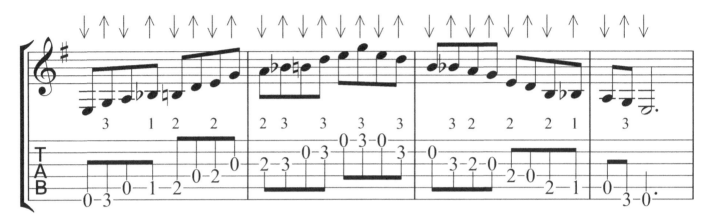

Exercise 24

Practice the G major scale using alternate picking.

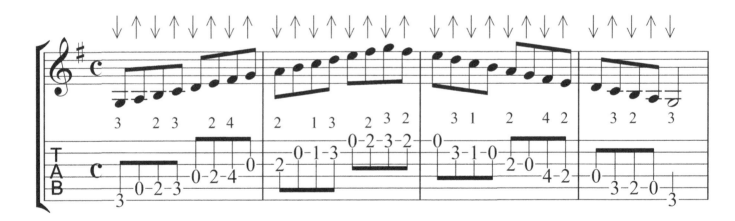

Exercise 25

Practice the Am scale using alternate picking.

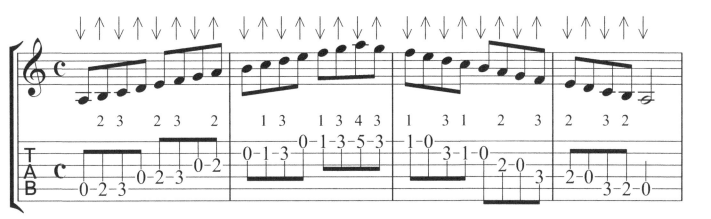

Exercise 26

Practice the chromatic scale using alternate picking.

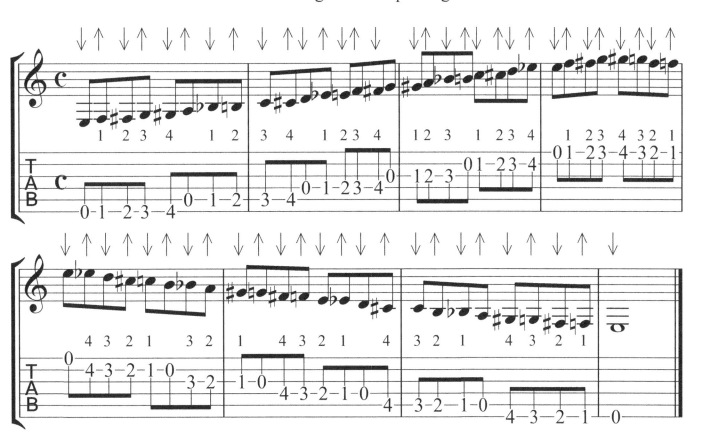

Section 3
Chord Progressions, Strumming, and Scales

To access Online Video & Audio for this course, go to the following internet address:

cvls.com/extras/begl

Chord Progression in G

In the next few exercises we will learn a few new chords and then put them together into a chord progression. *A chord progression is a series of chords*. Let's start by practicing the chords.

Exercise 27

Practice each one of these chords until they become familiar to you. Play towards the front of the frets and keep your thumb in a good position on the back of the neck. Strum each chord slowly and check each string for clarity.

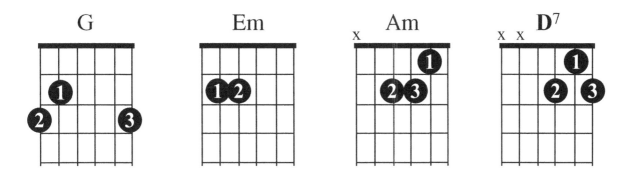

Exercise 28

When changing chords we will be using two extremely important techniques. The pivot finger, which we have seen earlier in this course, and the guide finger. A pivot finger is a finger that can remain exactly where it is from one chord to the next. *A guide finger is a finger that stays on the same string but must slide either up or down the neck* to get to the next chord. Changing from G to Em, the 1st finger is a pivot. From Em to Am, the 2nd finger is a pivot. From Am to D^7, the 1st finger is a pivot, and from D^7 back to G, the 3rd finger is a guide.

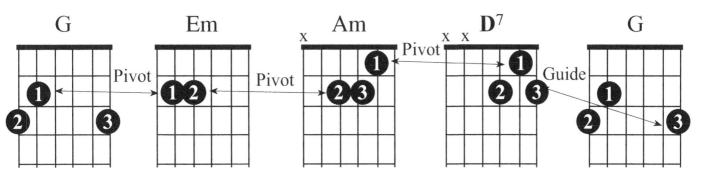

41

Playing with a Track

Now that we've practiced the chords and the chord changes, we can try playing along with a track. This will get us practicing playing in time and with a band.

Exercise 29

Practice each one of these chords until they become familiar to you. Play towards the front of the frets and keep your thumb in a good position on the back of the neck. Strum each chord slowly and check each string for clarity.

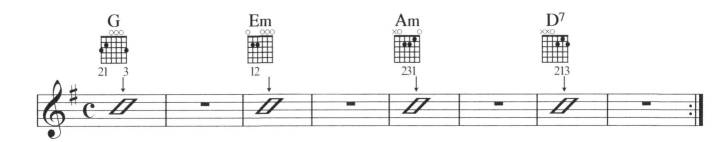

Exercise 30

We'll play the same chord progression with the track once more but this time with a different strum pattern. The pattern will be down up down. The trick to getting the strum directions correct is to stay in motion with the right hand. This is a small jump in difficulty and will get us to play more musically.

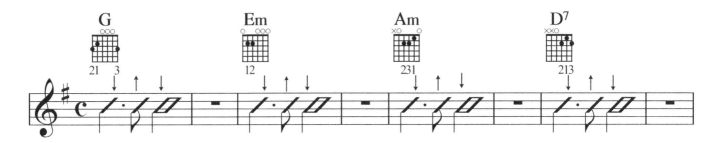

Muted Strumming 1

A great way to develop good technique and the right motion for strumming is the muted strumming drill. This exercise is one that you should hold on to and use as long as you play guitar. Remember, the guitar is primarily a percussion instrument so playing rhythm in time and with good feel is the most important thing a guitarist does.

In order to do this exercise we first must lay our left hand fingers across all the strings. Lightly touch the strings but don't press them down. It's like a piece of cloth is laying across the strings. If you press too hard you will hear notes which we don't want. The same will happen if you don't touch enough. After positioning your fingers test the sound by strumming the strings. They should all sound muted.

Let's go over some notations we will need to understand. The first note or downbeat in this example is a quarter note. It looks slightly different from standard music notation because we aren't notating a specific note to play but only a rhythm. A quarter note is one beat long. The symbols to the right of the quarter note are rests. This means don't play anything for these beats. On beat 1, we strum. Then, on beats 2, 3, and 4 we don't. The downward arrow means play beat one with a downstroke. Upward arrows would meant to play with an upstroke.

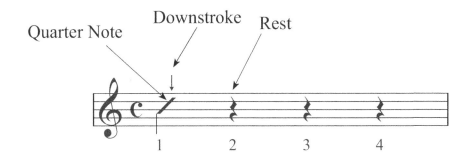

Exercise 31

Use muted strumming to play this rhythm. It is important to stay in motion with the right hand even when you are not playing anything on beats 2, 3, and 4. Continue the strumming motion with the right hand hovering over the strings but not actually playing them. Strum on beat 1 using a downstroke. This constant motion of our right hand will be our core strumming technique.

Exercise 32

In this example of muted strumming, strum on beats 1 and 3 with a downstroke. Stay in motion with your right hand on the other beats using constant motion. Keep your forearm and wrist moving together in a fluid relaxed fashion.

Eighth Notes

In order to play the next exercise, we will have to read eighth notes in our strumming pattern. Eighth notes in this example have a beam attaching them together. They are played twice as fast as quarter notes or two per beat. On beat two in the notation below, we play a downstroke. On the "and" of beat 2 we play an upstroke.

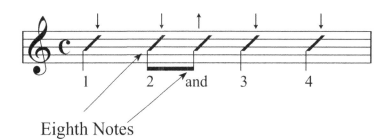

Eighth Notes

44

Exercise 33

In this exercise we will add upstrokes to our patterns. Count 1, 2 and 3, 4.
Remember eighth notes are twice as fast as quarters and pay attention to the arrows
for strumming direction. Stay in constant motion.

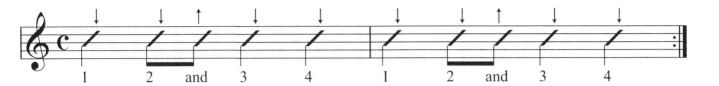

Muted Strumming 2

Now we'll add a little more complexity to our strumming patterns. Work your way through these patterns and they should become great exercises for you to use as you develop your guitar playing.

Exercise 34

In this exercise, we will add even more eighth notes to our pattern. Practice this pattern until is flows smoothly. Pay attention to the direction of the strums.

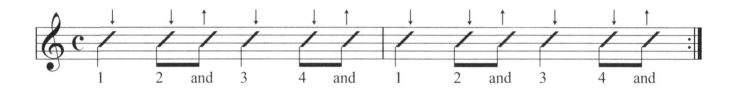

Exercise 35

This pattern is just a slight deviation of the last pattern and this time starts with eighth notes.

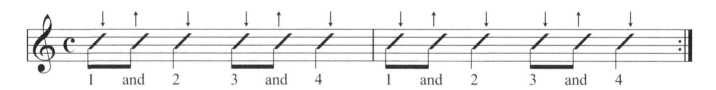

Exercise 36

In this exercise we add still more eighth notes.

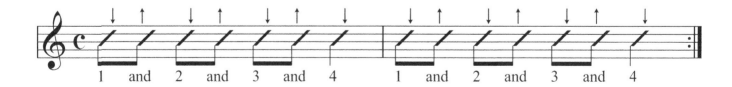

Exercise 37

In this exercise, we attach two patterns we have learned before into a longer pattern. Remember to stay in constant motion.

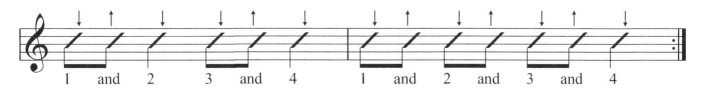

Strumming Patterns With Chords

Let's try using these same patterns while playing an Em chord. This will give us a chance to hear what these patterns sound like while making some music.

Exercise 38

Here is the pattern we learned in a previous exercise but this time try it with an Em chord.

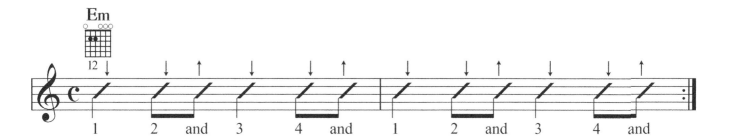

Exercise 39

Try this strum pattern while playing an Em chord.

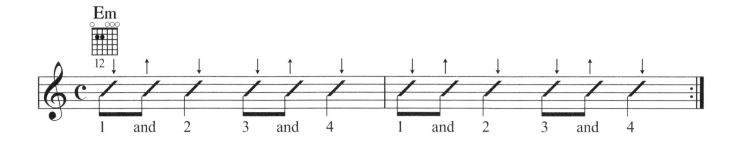

Exercise 40

One more pattern while playing an Em chord. Lots of eighth notes this time.

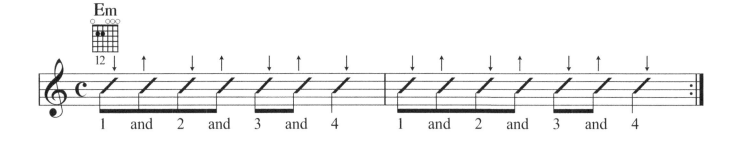

Exercise 41

Finally, with this exercise we play two patterns spliced together to make a longer one. Make sure the Em chord sounds clean and full by strumming all the strings.

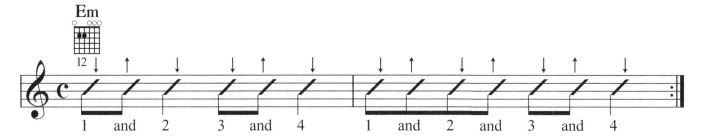

Am, Am⁷, FM⁷, E⁷ Chords

In this section, we will introduce several more chords. It is important at this point to begin increasing our chord vocabulary. We already know the A minor chord, but new chords will be A minor seven (Am^7), F major seven (FM^7), and E seven (E^7).

Exercise 42

Begin by practicing each one of these chords on their own. Notice that in the first three chords we are not strumming the sixth string. Practice each chord concentrating on good hand and finger position. Watch your thumb on the back of the neck and don't let it get too high. Play on the tips of your fingers towards the front of the frets and listen for clarity with each string.

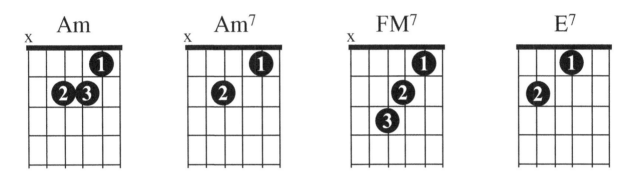

Exercise 43

Your first goal is to play each chord clearly. Once that is accomplished, start working on changing chords. When you change between Am and Am^7 you can leave fingers 1 and 2 in place (pivot fingers) and simply lift the 3rd finger. Try to make sure the open 3rd string isn't muted. From Am^7 to FM^7, leave the 1st finger still. From FM^7 to E^7, you will need to lift everything since there is no pivot or guide finger. Practice these chord changes. When you are ready, try playing along with the track.

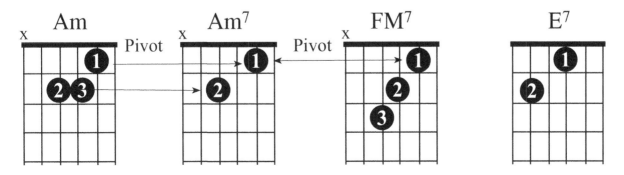

Am, Am⁷, FM⁷, E⁷ with Strum

Now let's try using these chords with a strum pattern.

Exercise 44

While playing this chord progression we will add a simple strum pattern. The pattern has two downstrokes to start it off and then a stop or mute with your right hand. To execute the mute bring your right hand to the strings and mute all of them. This is a rhythmic stop and should happen on beat three and then we should hear nothing on beats three and four. Think of it as Down, Down, Stop. Try saying it to yourself in time with the beat. When you are comfortable with this pattern, try playing along with the track.

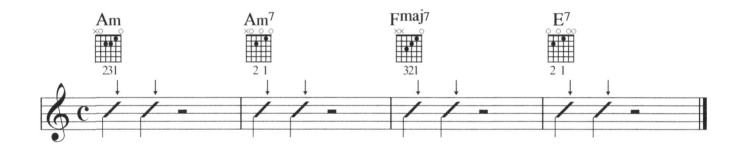

The Am Pentatonic Scale

Earlier in this course, we learned the E minor pentatonic scale and now let's increase our knowledge of scales and learn another pentatonic scale: the A minor pentatonic scale.

Exercise 45

Practice the A minor pentatonic scale as shown below. Pay attention to fingerings. Keep your thumb low on the back of the neck and play towards the front of the frets on the tips of your fingers. Use alternate picking.

Exercise 46

Now practice this same scale forwards and backwards. Don't repeat the highest note of the scale when you get there. Make sure to use alternate picking. When you are comfortable playing this scale, try practicing it in time along with the track.

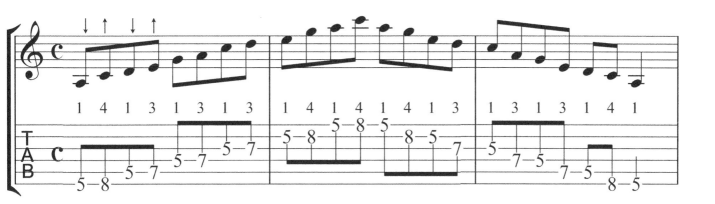

Stretching Exercises

In order to advance our guitar playing, it is important to gain some mobility and independence with our left hand fingers. These stretching exercises will speed up that process. As with any exercise, be careful when doing these stretches. Make sure your hands are warmed up and not cold. Never do a stretch until the point of pain. If you do feel pain, discontinue. If you have any injuries or disabilities in your wrists, hands, or arms you should be extra careful and double check with your doctor to make sure these are okay for you.

Exercise 45

In the next set of pictures, you will see a series of hand positions that gradually increase the stretch or expansion of the hand. Start with position 1 and place your hand and fingers in this position. The index finger is at the 7th fret the 2nd finger at the 8th fret, the 3rd finger is at the 9th fret and the 4th finger is at the 10th fret. Keep a low thumb placement and stay in this position for twenty to thirty seconds. Then shift your whole hand down one fret, as seen in position 2, and hold that position again for twenty to thirty seconds. Slide down the neck and hold each position. The frets get further apart as you slide down the neck. Only go as far as your hand can go to obtain a good stretch. Don't go too far and cause pain. Over time, gradually increase the amount of stretch by going further down the neck. The amount of stretch depends greatly on your hand size, so take your time.

Position 1. Index finger at 7th fret

Position 2. Index finger at 6th fret

Position 3. Index finger at 5th fret

Position 4. Index finger at 4th fret

Position 5. Index finger at 3rd fret

Position 6. Index finger at 2nd fret

Position 7. Index finger at 1st fret

Exercise 45

In these next series of pictures, you will see variations of the stretch we just learned. Execute each one the same as the previous stretches by holding each position for twenty to thirty seconds and working your way down the neck. Remember to take your time. These stretches may be difficult at first and it may take weeks or months to see significant progress. Remember, the goal is to get a good stretch and not necessarily to go all the way down the neck. Keep in mind that every hand size is different.

Stretch Variation 1

Stretch Variation 2

Stretch Variation 3

Stretch Variation 4

Conclusion

Congratulations on completing The Beginner Electric Guitar Course. I hope you have enjoyed learning to play the guitar. Continue your progress by going on to one of the suggestions listed here. Remember, a little bit of practice every day, will go a long way over time. My name is Peter Vogl and thanks for using this course.

More Books by Peter Vogl

The Guitarist's Chord Book by Peter Vogl is a 144 page book that contains over 900 chords with photos to clearly illustrate each chord and each note of the chord is labeled. This kindle edition makes finding chords you want to play easy. It also contains a special moveable chords section with the most widely used shapes for each class of chord. Peter Vogl has also included goodies from his bag of tricks to give you new sounds, shapes, and inspirations for song arrangements. The chord shapes have been reviewed by guitar teachers and players across the country. This is a must read for guitar players of all levels

The Guitarist's Scale Book by Peter Vogl is a complete scale encyclopedia for guitar with over 400 scales and modes. It contains scale diagrams with notation and tablature for each scale and tips on how and when to use each scale.

This scale book also contains outside jazz scales, exotic scales, Peter's own Cross-Stringing scales, and easy to understand explanations of scales and modes. This is the only guitar scale book you'll ever need.

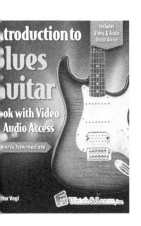

The *Introduction to Blues Guitar Book* by Peter Vogl is a beginning to intermediate course that will teach you the essential concepts of rhythm and soloing for blues guitar. We'll start by learning chords and strum patterns to play over several distinct rhythms and progressions (slow, shuffle, swing, minor). Peter will also cover the 12-bar blues form and show you a series of turnarounds. From there, we'll move on to soloing in the key of E before moving on to other keys. You'll learn how to play, understand, and use a series of scales. Finally, Peter will provide detailed instruction on playing 7 different beginner solos. Each of the solos will show you how to add techniques and phrasing to your lead playing. This course also includes online access to video lessons and audio jam tracks so you can practice each exercise, song, and solo in context.

These products are available on Amazon.com. If you have any questions, problems, or comments, please contact us at:

Watch & Learn, Inc.
2947 East Point St.
East Point, GA 30344
800-416-7088
sales@cvls.com

Made in the USA
Columbia, SC
21 April 2021